## Ways to Go

# BIKES GO!

By Sean MacDumont

Gareth Stevens
PUBLISHING

**Please visit our website, www.garethstevens.com. For a free color catalog of all our high-quality books, call toll free 1-800-542-2595 or fax 1-877-542-2596.**

**Cataloging-in-Publication Data**

Names: MacDumont, Sean.
Title: Bikes go! / Sean MacDumont.
Description: New York : Gareth Stevens Publishing, 2018. | Series: Ways to go | Includes index.
Identifiers: ISBN 9781538210093 (pbk.) | ISBN 9781538210116 (library bound) | ISBN 9781538210109 (6 pack)
Subjects: LCSH: Bicycles–Juvenile literature. | Cycling–Juvenile literature.
Classification: LCC TL412.M33 2018 | DDC 629.227'2–dc23

First Edition

Published in 2018 by
**Gareth Stevens Publishing**
111 East 14th Street, Suite 349
New York, NY 10003



Editor: Kate Mikoley
Designer: Sam DeMartin

Photo credits: Cover, pp. 1, 21 Sergey Novikov/Shutterstock.com; pp. 5, 23 Monkey Business Images/Shutterstock.com; p. 7 fotum/Shutterstock.com; pp. 9, 24 (wheel) greenland/Shutterstock.com; p. 11 Anna Grigorjeva/Shutterstock.com; p. 13 Pressmaster/Shutterstock.com; p. 15, 24 (brake) Rob Byron/Shutterstock.com; pp. 17, 24 (helmet) MNStudio/Shutterstock.com; p. 19 Dasha Rosato/Shutterstock.com.



Printed in the United States of America

CPSIA compliance information: Batch #CW18GS: For further information contact Gareth Stevens, New York, New York at 1-800-542-2595.

# Contents

We can go with bikes!

People ride bikes.
Their feet make
the bike go.

Bikes have two wheels.

wheels

Your hands help you turn.

Bikes can go fast.

Brakes make the bike stop.

brake

Helmets keep you safe.
They go on your head.

Bikes are faster than walking.

You can ride your bike to school.

You can ride your bike around the park.

# Words to Know

brakes

helmet

wheel

# Index